You Will Never HAVE THIS DAY Again

A Collection of INSPIRATION and BEAUTY

FALL
RIVER
PRESS

New York

FALL RIVER PRESS

New York

An Imprint of Sterling Publishing Co., Inc.
1166 Avenue of the Americas
New York, NY 10036

ISBN 978-1-4351-6634-9

For information about custom editions, special sales, and premium
and corporate purchases, please contact Sterling Special Sales at
800-805-5489 or specialsales@sterlingpublishing.com.

Manufactured in China

10 9 8 7 6 5 4 3 2

www.sterlingpublishing.com

Jacket and Interior Design © Tandem Books, Inc.
Front Jacket Photo © PHOTOCREO Michal Bednarek/Shutterstock.com
Back Jacket Photo © Teeraphan Pensupha/Shutterstock.com
Endpaper Photo © volodimir bazyuk/Shutterstock.com
Image Credits—See Last Page

YOU WILL NEVER HAVE THIS DAY AGAIN!

That's true of all days, but as we go through our everyday routines, it's easy to forget. It's easy to take the good and the bad for granted, to put your dreams on the shelf for the sake of the day-to-day, to overlook the beauty all around. Sometimes, though, just hearing a turn of phrase, a bit of wit and wisdom at the right moment, can reopen your eyes and your mind to the wonders around you—and the wonders inside yourself.

In *You Will Never Have This Day Again*, inspiring quotes and truisms are paired with uplifting photography from around the world to serve as reminders for what you know in your heart to be true but can lose sight of in your workaday life. They act as guideposts to help you find your way through hardship. They help motivate when your load feels heavy and the road is long. They assure that you are not alone in your struggles, nor are you alone in your joys. They are spiritual buoys, imparting inspiration for when you are low and reminding you to spread love and happiness when you have it in abundance.

Some sayings will resonate with your heart, others with your mind. Take the gifts from this treasury as they come and spread them as you will. They are benefactions from people across the centuries and around the globe—both lauded and famous, and unsung and anonymous. Please enjoy these pages and let them serve as comfort, inspiration, and reassurance on your journey.

SOME DAYS
YOU HAVE TO CREATE
YOUR OWN SUNSHINE.

WHEN SOMETHING GOES WRONG IN YOUR LIFE,

JUST YELL

"PLOT TWIST!"

AND MOVE ON.

LIFE ISN'T ABOUT WAITING

for the storm to pass,

IT'S ABOUT LEARNING

to dance in the rain.

— VIVIAN GREENE

You cannot save people,
you can only love them.

—Anaïs Nin

The best way
to make your
DREAMS COME TRUE
is to wake up.

—Paul Valéry

I AM NOT WHAT HAS *happened* TO ME.
I AM WHAT I *choose* TO BECOME.

—Carl Jung

Beauty begins the moment you decide *to be yourself.*

—Coco Chanel

Inhale

THE FUTURE.

Exhale

THE PAST.

WORK HARD

STAY HUMBLE

BE KIND

I NEVER LOSE.
EITHER I WIN
OR
I LEARN.

Never put
the key to your
happiness
in somebody
else's pocket.

—Tom Ziglar

We either make ourselves miserable or we make ourselves strong. The amount of work is the same.

—Carlos Castaneda

Your mistakes don't define you.

IF IT DOESN'T **CHALLENGE** YOU, IT WON'T **CHANGE** YOU.

—Zig Ziglar

STARS CAN'T SHINE
WITHOUT DARKNESS.

She believed
she *could*,
so she *did*.

Don't look back.
You're not going
that way.

DO I NOT DESTROY MY ENEMIES WHEN I MAKE THEM MY FRIENDS?

—Abraham Lincoln

IN THE END,
WE ONLY REGRET THE CHANCES WE DIDN'T TAKE.

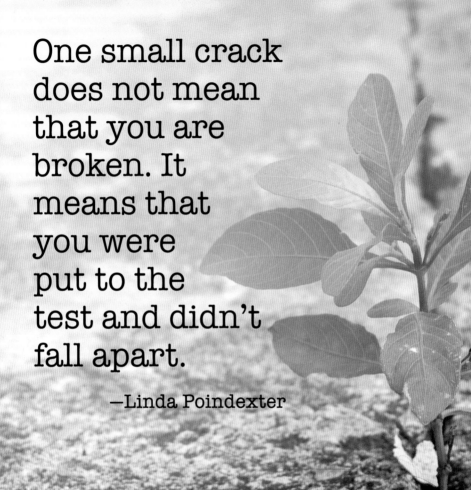

One small crack does not mean that you are broken. It means that you were put to the test and didn't fall apart.

—Linda Poindexter

YOU ONLY FAIL

WHEN YOU

STOP TRYING.

The problem is
not the PROBLEM.
The problem is
YOUR ATTITUDE
about the problem.

—Captain Jack Sparrow

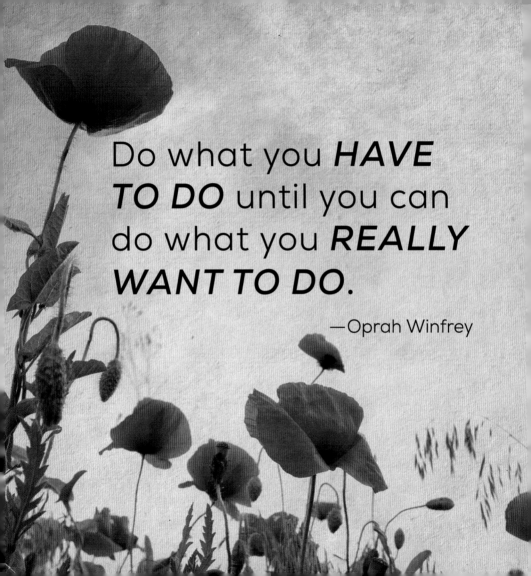

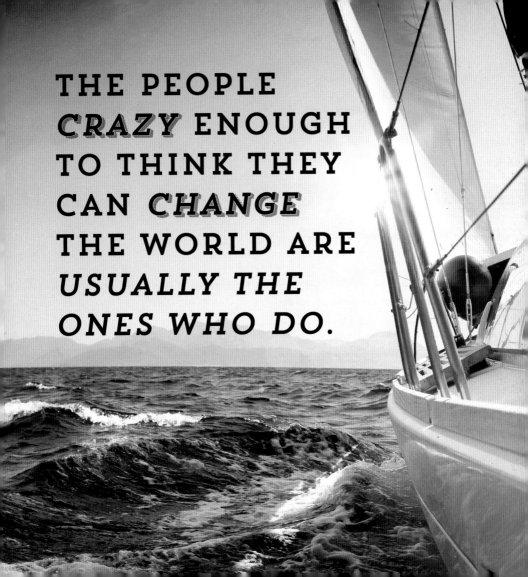

THE PEOPLE CRAZY ENOUGH TO THINK THEY CAN CHANGE THE WORLD ARE USUALLY THE ONES WHO DO.

What you GET by achieving your goals is not as important as WHAT YOU BECOME by achieving your goals.

—Zig Ziglar

DON'T WORRY ABOUT THOSE WHO TALK BEHIND YOUR BACK. THEY'RE BEHIND YOU FOR A REASON.

Just breathe.

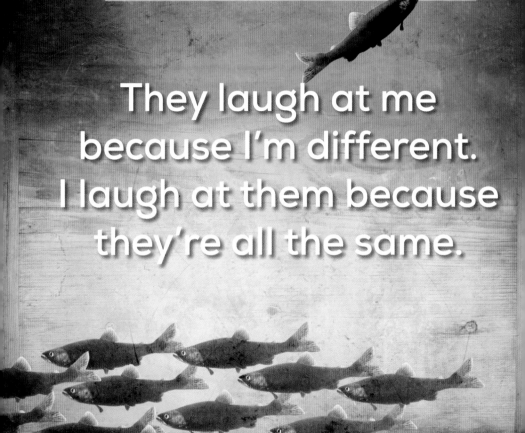

WORRYING DOESN'T TAKE AWAY TOMORROW'S TROUBLE, IT TAKES AWAY TODAY'S PEACE.

Creativity is
intelligence
having fun.

You have to take risks. We will only understand the miracle of life fully when we allow the unexpected to happen.

—Paulo Coelho

WHOEVER IS TRYING TO BRING YOU DOWN IS ALREADY BELOW YOU.

You must learn a new way to *think* before you can master a new way to *be*.

—Marianne Williamson

To thine own self

BE TRUE.

—*Hamlet*

Character is how you treat those who can do nothing for you.

You can't start
the next chapter
of your life if you
keep re-reading the
last one.

DO NOT JUDGE ME BY MY SUCCESSES, JUDGE ME BY HOW MANY TIMES I FELL DOWN AND GOT BACK UP AGAIN.

— NELSON MANDELA

MARCH TO YOUR OWN BEAT.

Spread love everywhere you go.
Let no one ever come to you
without leaving happier.

—Mother Teresa

STRESS happens when you try to control the world around you. RELAX and remember the only real control you have is over yourself.

Courage is the knowledge of the grounds of hope and fear.

—Plato

If there is no struggle,
there is no progress.

—Frederick Douglass

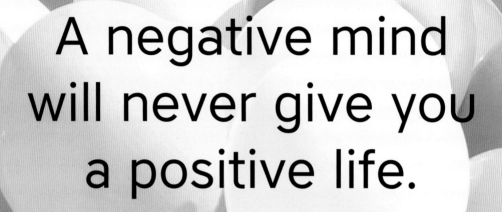

A negative mind will never give you a positive life.

—*Ziad K. Abdelnour*

When you can't control what's happening, control the way you respond to it. THAT'S WHAT *POWER* IS.

Sometimes when things are falling apart, they may actually be falling into place.

TACT IS THE ART OF MAKING A POINT WITHOUT MAKING AN ENEMY.

—Howard W. Newton

Never get so busy
making a living that
you forget to make a life.

What are you reacting to?
Ask yourself that question
every moment of every
day when your peace is
disturbed.

—Kenneth Wapnick

EVERYONE YOU WILL EVER MEET KNOWS SOMETHING YOU DON'T.

—Bill Nye

You get in life what you have the courage to ask for.

—Oprah Winfrey

The one who falls and gets up is so much stronger than the one who never fell.

BE KIND.
FOR EVERYONE YOU MEET
IS FIGHTING A BATTLE YOU
KNOW NOTHING ABOUT.

Shoot for the moon. Even if you miss, you'll land among the stars.

—Les Brown

I DID NOT KNOW WHAT I WANTED TO DO BUT I KNEW THE KIND OF WOMAN I WANTED TO BE.

—DIANE VON FURSTENBERG

Inhale confidence.
Exhale doubt.

The best way to
get things done is
to simply begin.

Don't waste words on people
who deserve your silence.

If "Plan A" doesn't work, the alphabet has twenty-five more letters.

DON'T RUIN A GOOD TODAY BY THINKING ABOUT A BAD YESTERDAY.

Either you run the day
or the day runs you.

—J. C. McPheeters

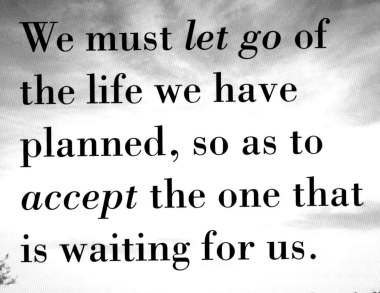

We must *let go* of the life we have planned, so as to *accept* the one that is waiting for us.

—Joseph Campbell

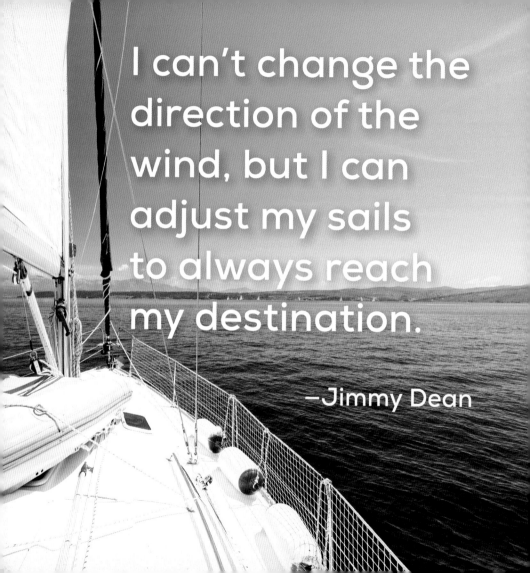

Nothing is impossible, the word itself says "I'm possible"!

—Audrey Hepburn

What you are comes to you.

—Ralph Waldo Emerson

What we think,
we become.

Keep your face to the sunshine and you can never see the shadow.

—Helen Keller

There are two ways of spreading light: to be the candle or the mirror that reflects it.

—Edith Wharton

NO ACT OF KINDNESS, NO MATTER

HOW SMALL, IS EVER WASTED.

—AESOP

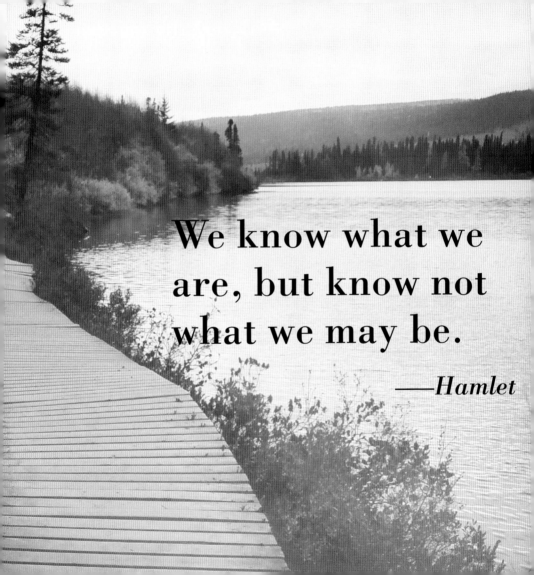

We know what we are, but know not what we may be.

——*Hamlet*

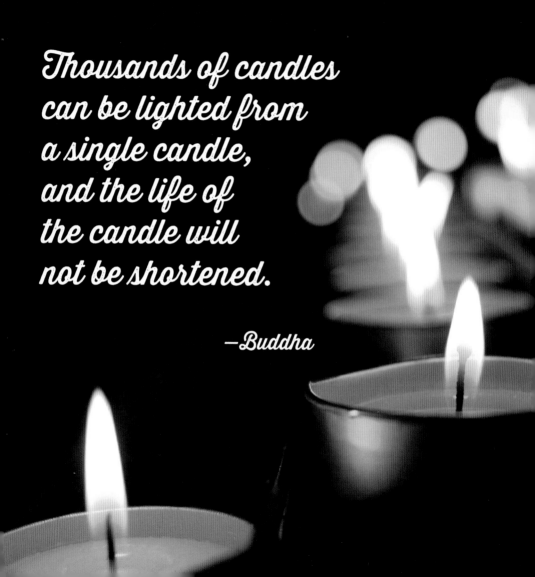

HOW WONDERFUL IT IS
THAT NOBODY NEED
WAIT A SINGLE MOMENT
BEFORE STARTING TO
IMPROVE THE WORLD.

—ANNE FRANK

WHEN WE SEEK TO DISCOVER THE
BEST IN OTHERS, WE SOMEHOW BRING
OUT THE BEST IN OURSELVES.

—WILLIAM ARTHUR WARD

TWO ROADS DIVERGED IN A WOOD AND I—
I TOOK THE ONE LESS TRAVELED BY,
AND THAT HAS MADE ALL THE DIFFERENCE.

—Robert Frost

One today is worth
two tomorrows.

—Benjamin Franklin

If I have seen farther than others, it is because I was standing on the shoulders of giants.

–Isaac Newton

DON'T JUDGE EACH DAY BY THE HARVEST YOU REAP BUT BY THE SEEDS THAT YOU PLANT.

—ROBERT LOUIS STEVENSON

WELL-BEHAVED WOMEN
SELDOM MAKE HISTORY.

—Laurel Thatcher Ulrich

I will no longer accept the things
I cannot change, but rather change
the things I cannot accept.

There is nothing
stronger in
the world than
gentleness.

—Han Suyin

The size of the audience doesn't matter.

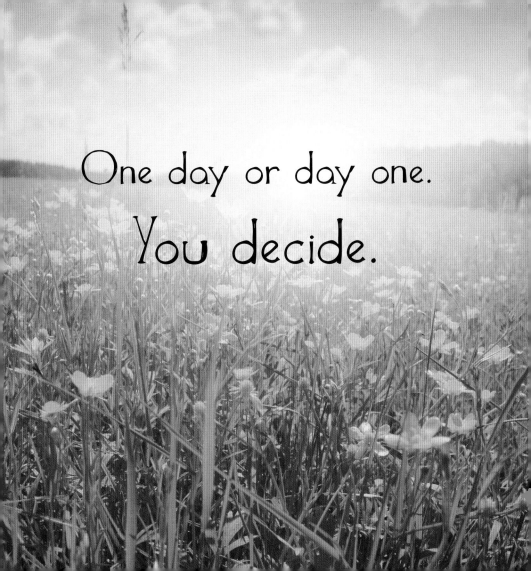

A goal *should* scare you a little and excite you a lot.

—Joe Vitale

EVERY ACCOMPLISHMENT BEGINS WITH THE DECISION TO TRY.

LIFE WILL ONLY CHANGE WHEN YOU BECOME MORE COMMITTED TO YOUR DREAMS THAN YOU ARE TO YOUR COMFORT ZONE.

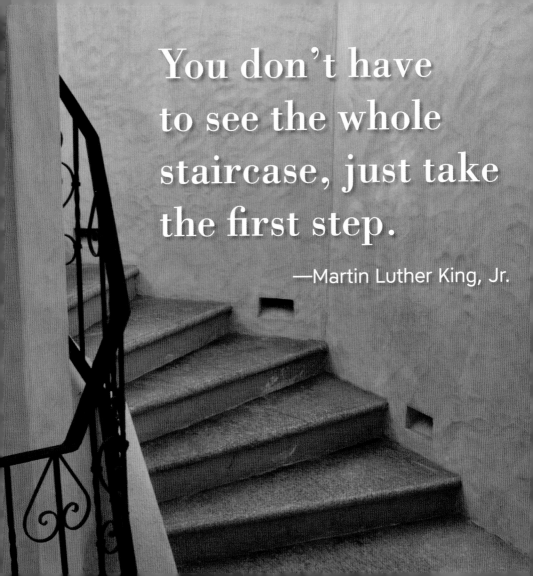

You don't have
to see the whole
staircase, just take
the first step.

—Martin Luther King, Jr.

This is my life . . . my story . . . my book. I will no longer let anyone else write it, nor will I apologize for the edits I make. —Steve Maraboli

NO AMOUNT OF *GUILT* CAN CHANGE THE PAST. NO AMOUNT OF *ANXIETY* CAN CHANGE THE FUTURE.

STRESS, ANXIETY, AND *DEPRESSION* ARE CAUSED WHEN WE ARE LIVING TO PLEASE OTHERS.

—Paulo Coelho

What you
give power
to has power
over you.

Never assume that **LOUD *is* STRONG** and **QUIET *is* WEAK.**

LET YOUR SMILE
CHANGE THE
WORLD,
BUT DON'T
LET THE
WORLD CHANGE
YOUR SMILE.

Work hard in silence.
Let your success
be the noise.

YOU'VE GOT THIS!

FALLING DOWN
IS AN ACCIDENT.

STAYING DOWN
IS A CHOICE.

NEVER LET
THE THINGS YOU WANT
MAKE YOU FORGET
THE THINGS YOU HAVE.

The darkest nights produce the brightest stars.

IT ALWAYS SEEMS
IMPOSSIBLE . . .
UNTIL IT'S DONE.

TO LIVE IS THE RAREST THING IN THE WORLD. MOST PEOPLE EXIST, THAT IS ALL.

—OSCAR WILDE

Will it be easy?

Nope.

Will it be worth it?

Absolutely.

You must be the change you wish to see in the world.

— MAHATMA GANDHI

LIFE IS TOUGH, BUT NOT AS TOUGH AS YOU.

It's okay to be SCARED. Being scared means you're about to do something really, really BRAVE.

You don't
owe anyone
an explanation.

We're all building
our world, *right now,*
in real time.
Let's build it better.

—Lindy West

Do what you feel in your heart to be right, for you'll be criticized anyway.

—Eleanor Roosevelt

The future depends entirely on what each of us does every day; a movement is only people moving.

—Gloria Steinem

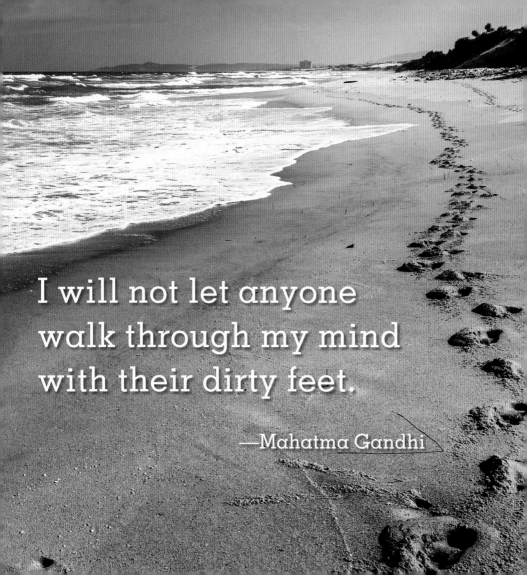

I will not let anyone walk through my mind with their dirty feet.

—Mahatma Gandhi

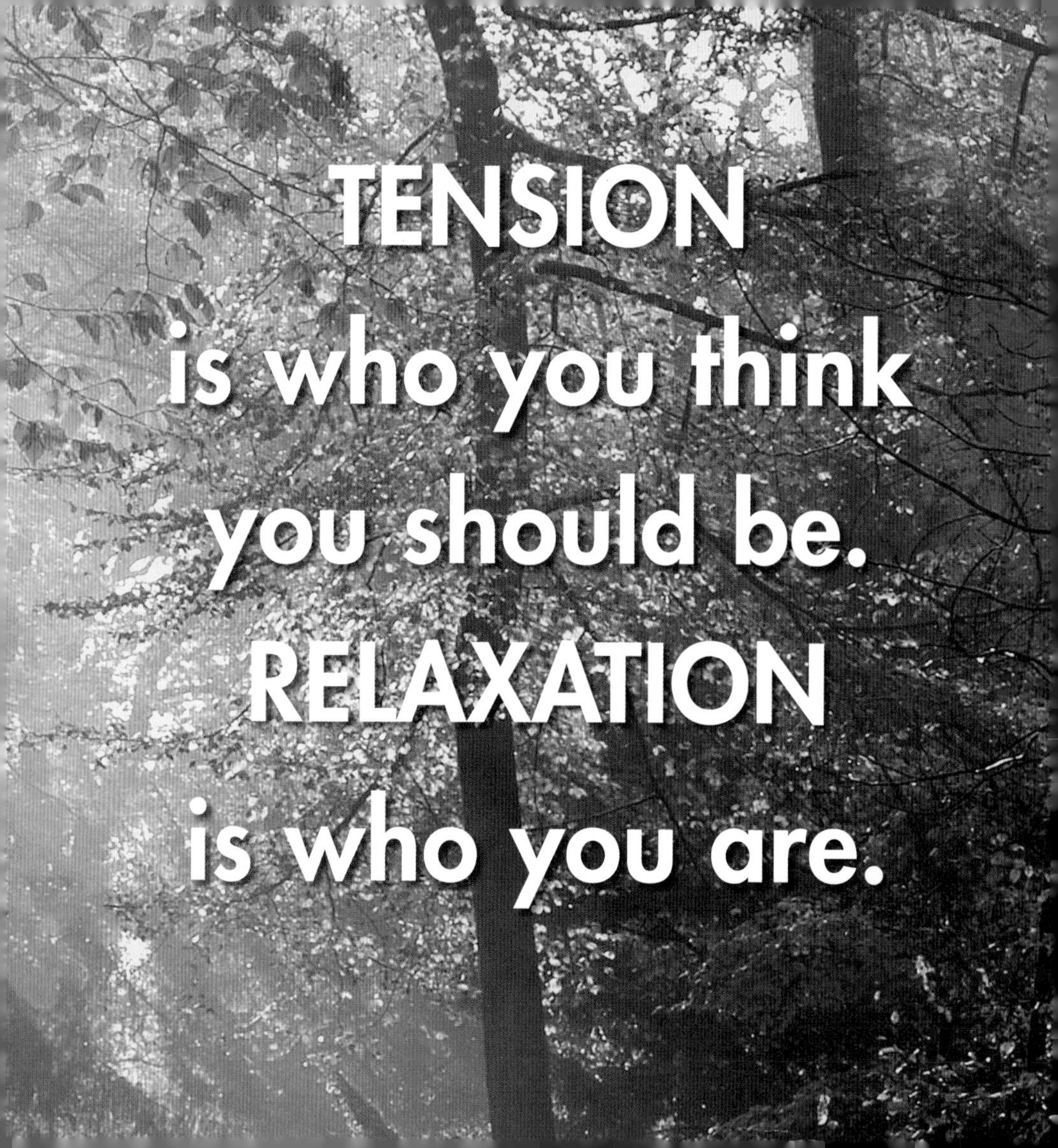
TENSION
is who you think
you should be.
RELAXATION
is who you are.

Some people say
you are going
the wrong way,
when it's simply
a way of your own.

—Angelina Jolie

DO WHAT YOU CAN, WITH WHAT YOU HAVE, WHERE YOU ARE.

— THEODORE ROOSEVELT

Be yourself; everyone else is already taken.

—Oscar Wilde

That's one small step for a man,
one giant leap for mankind.

—Neil Armstrong

I STILL BELIEVE, IN SPITE OF EVERYTHING, THAT PEOPLE ARE TRULY GOOD AT HEART.

—Anne Frank

One child,
one teacher,
one book and
one pen can
change the world.

—Malala Yousafzai

Figure out who you are and then do it on purpose.

-Dolly Parton

TO *FIND*
YOURSELF,
THINK FOR
YOURSELF.

—Socrates

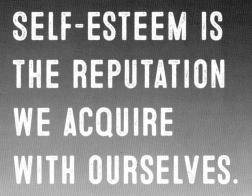

SELF-ESTEEM IS
THE REPUTATION
WE ACQUIRE
WITH OURSELVES.

—NATHANIEL BRANDEN

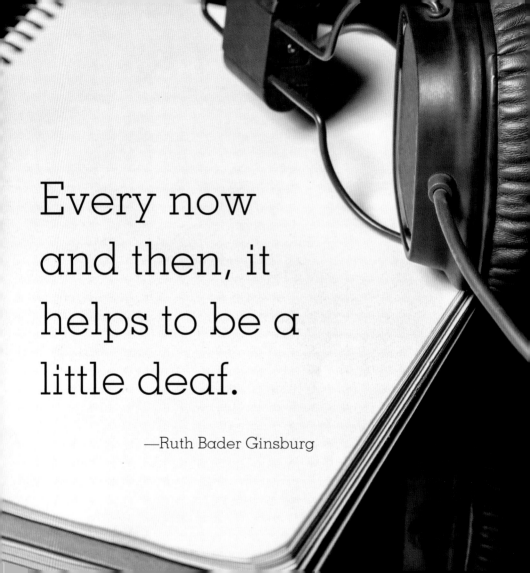

Every now and then, it helps to be a little deaf.

—Ruth Bader Ginsburg

Don't compromise yourself. You're all you've got.

—Janis Joplin

THERE IS A GREAT DEAL OF UNMAPPED COUNTRY WITHIN.

—GEORGE ELIOT

WHEN WE CANNOT
GET WHAT WE LIKE,
LET US LIKE WHAT
WE CAN GET.

—SPANISH PROVERB

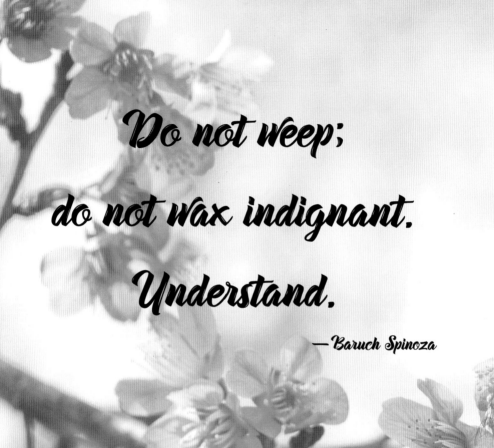

Do not weep;

do not wax indignant.

Understand.

— Baruch Spinoza

WE ARE WHAT WE REPEATEDLY DO. EXCELLENCE, THEN, IS NOT AN ACT, BUT A HABIT.

—Aristotle

The greater the obstacle, the more glory in overcoming it.

—Jean-Baptiste Molière

You miss
100 PERCENT
of the shots
you NEVER take.

—Wayne Gretzky

AS YOU THINK,
SO SHALL YOU BECOME.

PROBLEMS ARE ONLY OPPORTUNITIES IN WORK CLOTHES.

—HENRY KAISER

YOU WON'T
KNOW YOUR OWN
STRENGTH UNTIL
YOU HAVE TO
USE IT.

The troubles that chase you away also show you the road.

TOUGH TIMES NEVER LAST,
BUT TOUGH PEOPLE DO!

—ROBERT H. SCHULLER

It's the irritation
of life which
creates pearls.

—Larry Chang

I can, and I will.

IF YOU'RE CARRIED, YOU CAN'T APPRECIATE THE DISTANCE OF THE JOURNEY.

—AFRICAN PROVERB

When eating fruit,
think of the person
who planted the tree.

—Vietnamese proverb

No one can make you feel inferior without your consent.

—Eleanor Roosevelt

The best way to make your **dreams come true** is to wake up.

—Paul Valéry

LET US NOT
LOOK BACK IN ANGER,
OR FORWARD IN
FEAR, BUT AROUND
IN AWARENESS.

—James Thurber

Whatever you put your attention on will grow stronger in your life.

—Deepak Chopra

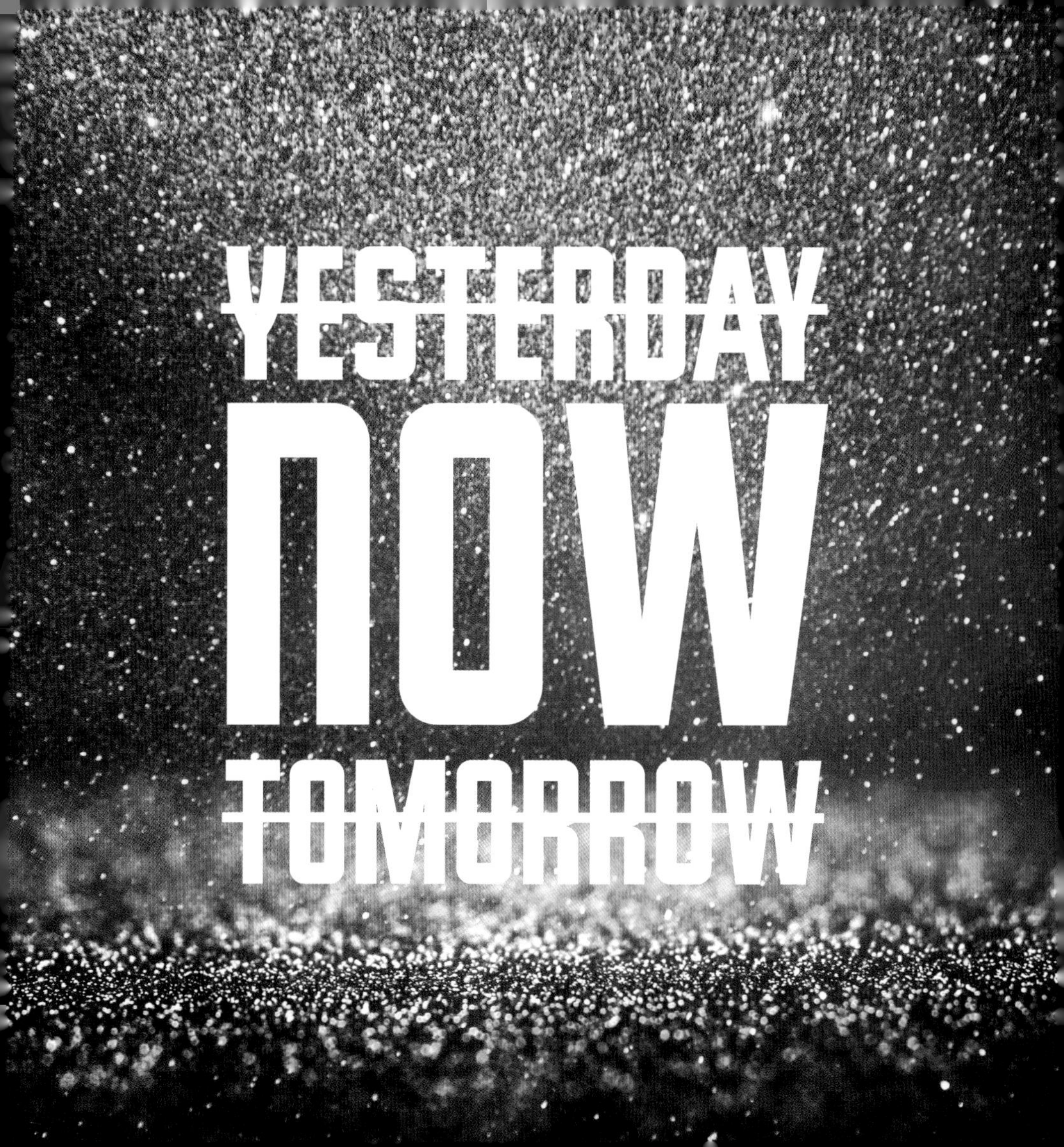
~~YESTERDAY~~
NOW
~~TOMORROW~~

IT'S NOT THE LOAD
THAT BREAKS YOU
DOWN, IT'S THE
WAY YOU CARRY IT.

—LENA HORNE

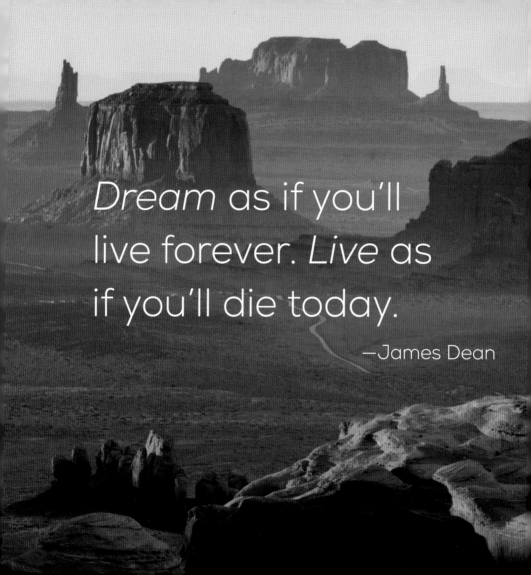

Dream as if you'll live forever. *Live* as if you'll die today.

—James Dean

If you can't change your fate, change your attitude.

—Amy Tan

FREEDOM IS THE CONTROL OF ONESELF.

IF YOU DON'T RUN YOUR OWN LIFE, SOMEONE ELSE WILL.

—JOHN ATKINSON

You cannot fix what
you will not face.

—James Baldwin

WHERE THERE IS SUNSHINE THERE IS ALSO SHADE.

— KASHMIRI PROVERB

Keep your eyes on the STARS, and your feet on the GROUND.

—Theodore Roosevelt

You can never cross the ocean unless you have the courage to lose sight of the shore.

—André Gide

BE SO GOOD
THEY CAN'T
IGNORE YOU.

–STEVE MARTIN

Throw kindness around like confetti.

You only fail
when you quit.

Grow antennae, not horns.

—James Angell

STARS ARE ONLY SPARKED IN THE DARK.

BELIEVE.

ACHIEVE.

REPEAT.

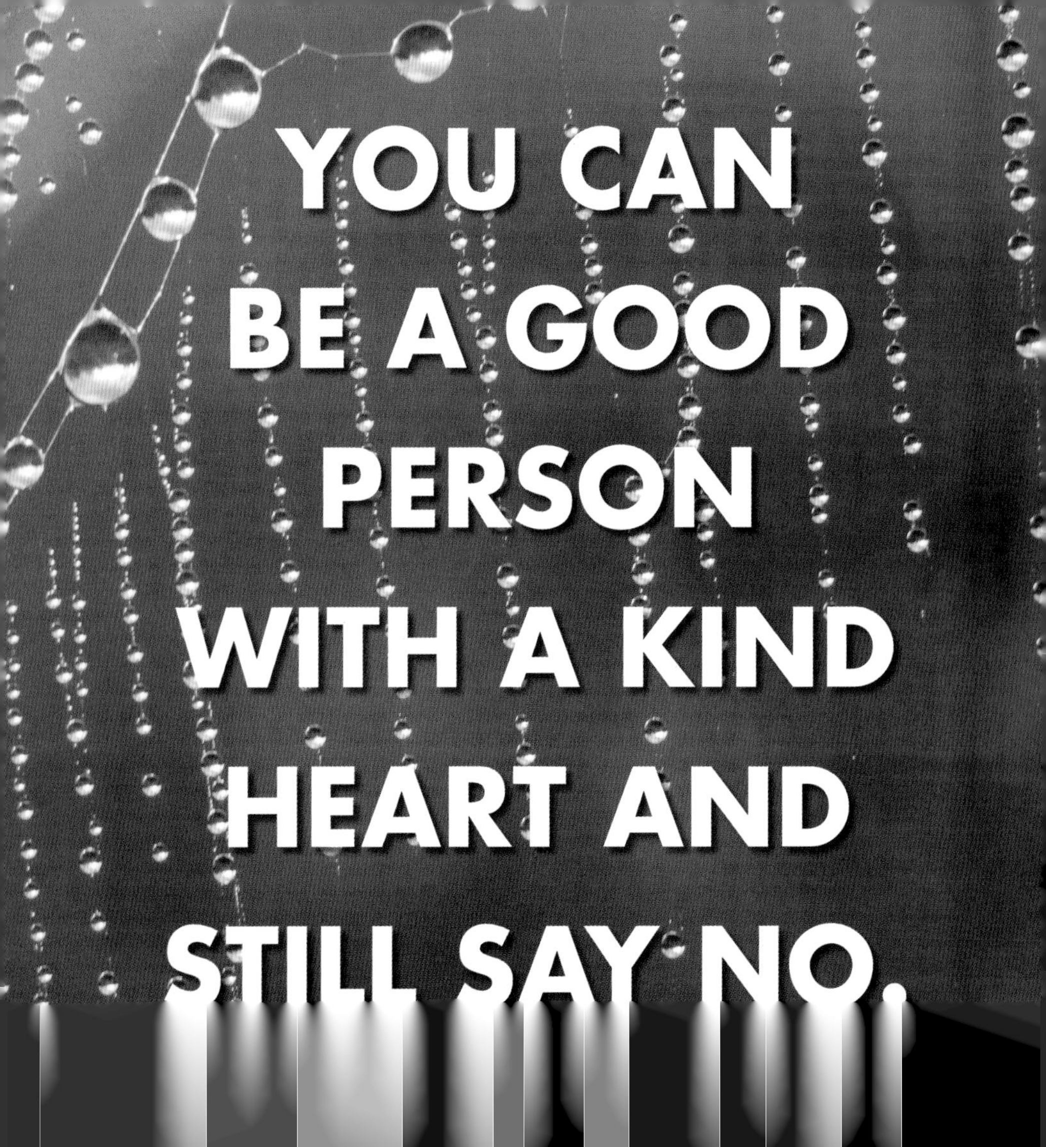
YOU CAN
BE A GOOD
PERSON
WITH A KIND
HEART AND
STILL SAY NO.

Every master was once a beginner.

IF YOU THINK YOU CAN DO A THING *OR* THINK YOU CAN'T DO A THING, *YOU'RE RIGHT.*

— HENRY FORD

Use today to
ensure that one
day you can say,
"I did it."

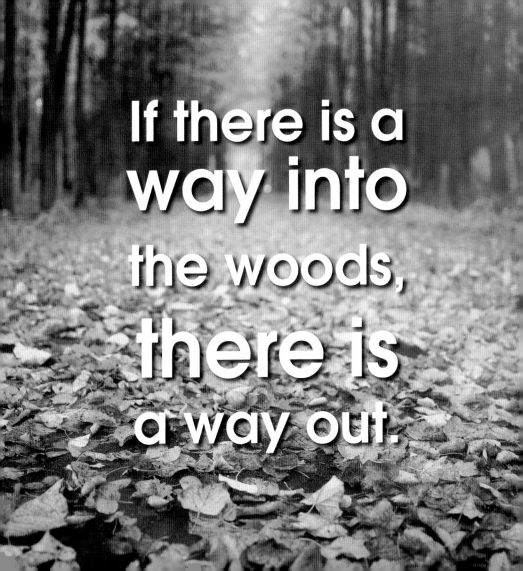

If there is a way into the woods, there is a way out.

A journey of a THOUSAND MILES must begin with a SINGLE STEP.

—Lao-tzu

WELL BEGUN IS HALF DONE.

— ARISTOTLE

Be willing to be
a beginner every
single morning.

—Meister Eckhart

If the first button of one's coat is wrongly buttoned, all the rest will be crooked.

—Giordano Bruno

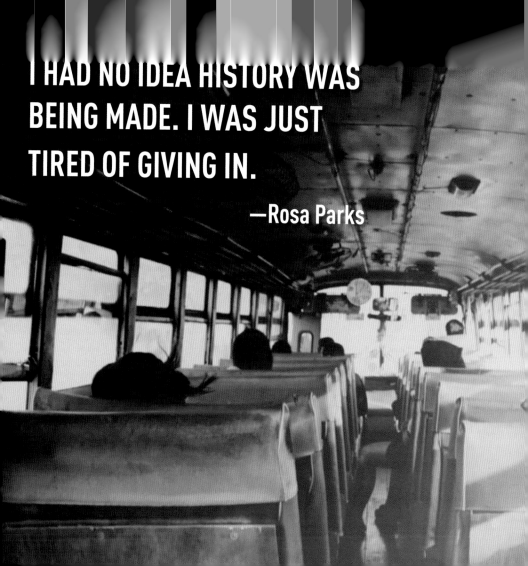

I HAD NO IDEA HISTORY WAS BEING MADE. I WAS JUST TIRED OF GIVING IN.

—Rosa Parks

Every beginning is a consequence— *every beginning ends something.*

—Paul Valéry

There are thousands of reasons why you cannot do what you want to.
All you need is one reason why you can.

-Willis R. Whitney

THINGS DO
NOT HAPPEN.
THINGS
ARE MADE
TO HAPPEN.

—John F. Kennedy

Knowing what you want is the first step toward getting it.

—Mae West

When they go LOW, we go HIGH.

—Michelle Obama

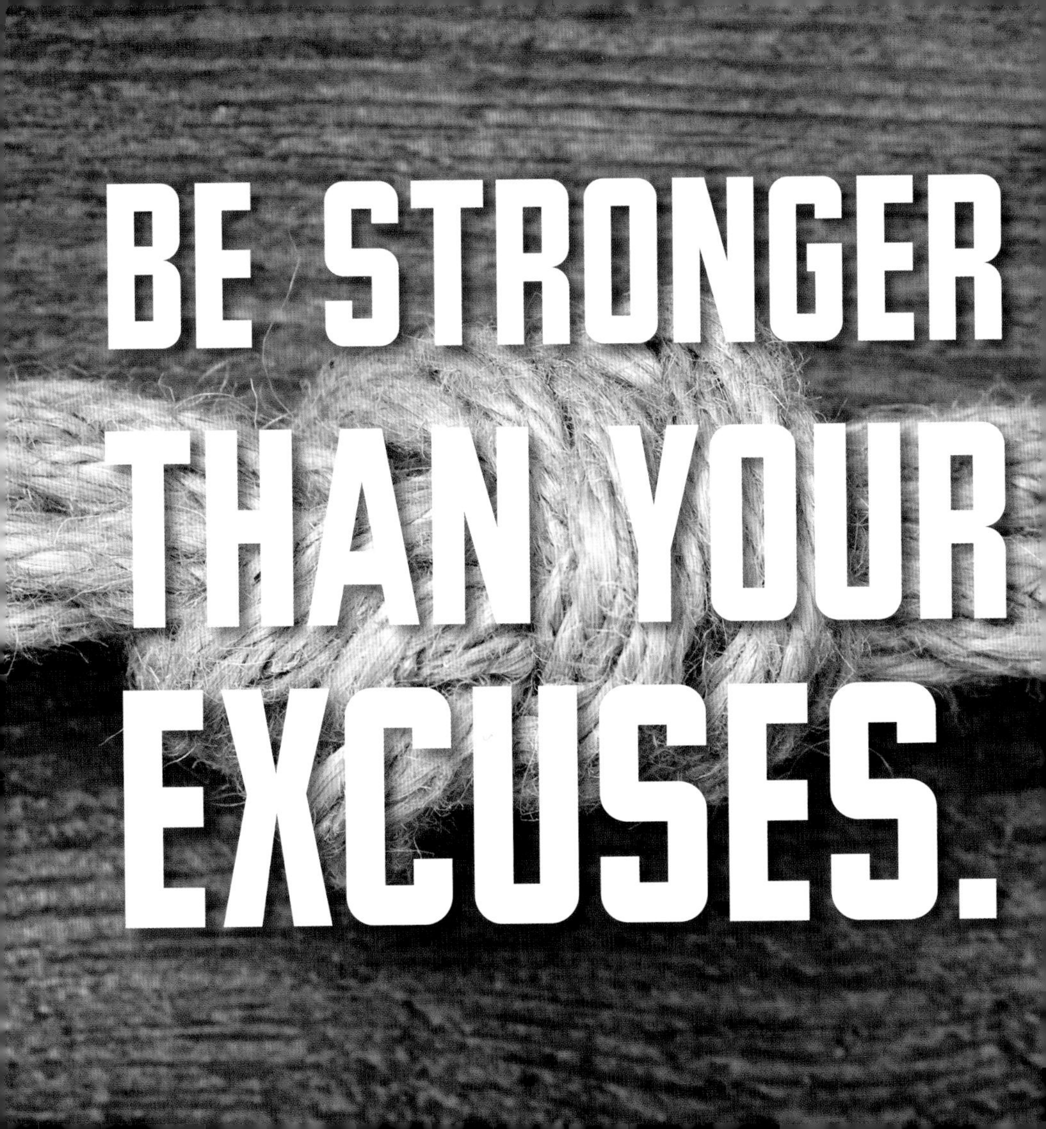
BE STRONGER
THAN YOUR
EXCUSES.

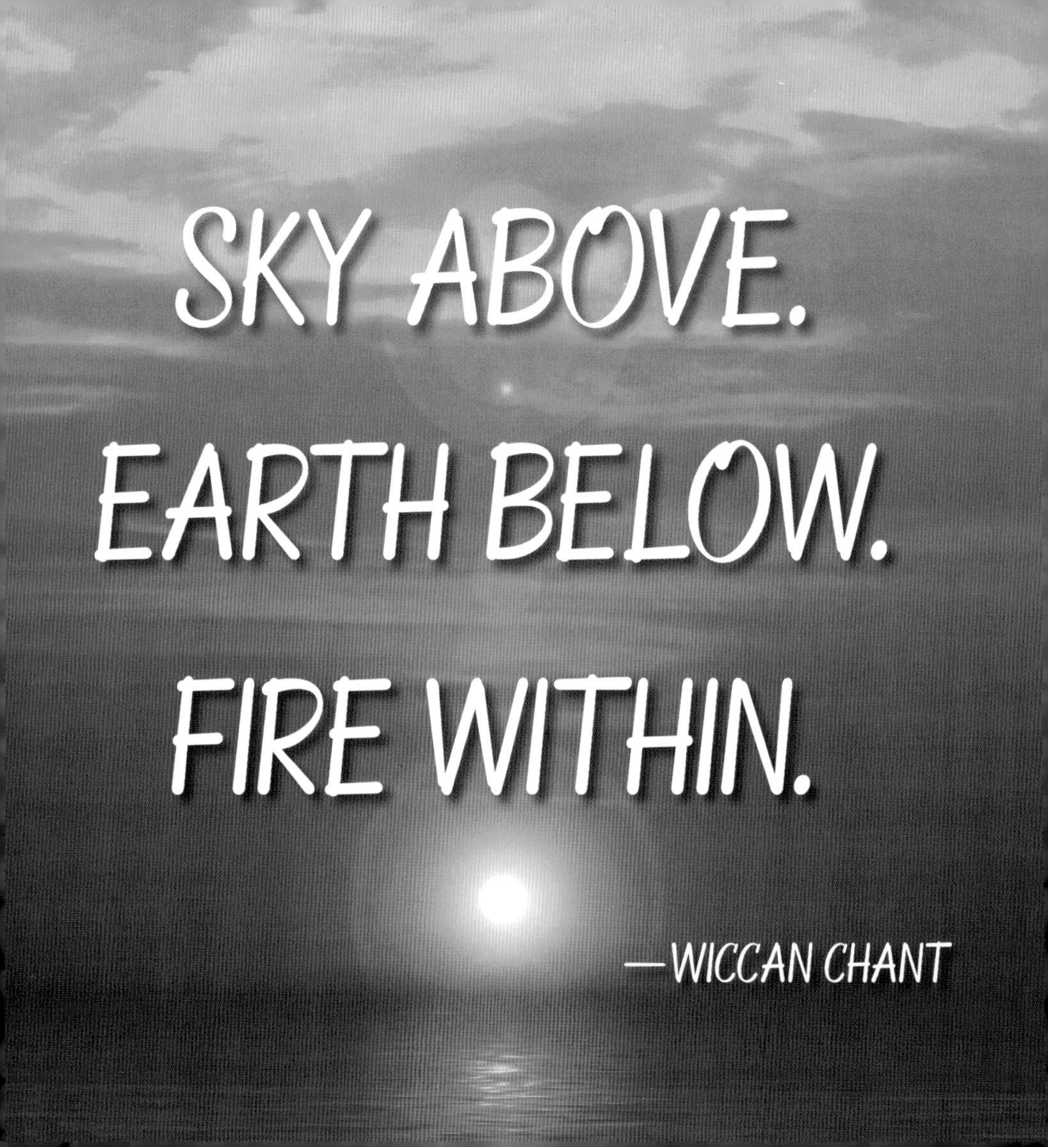
SKY ABOVE.
EARTH BELOW.
FIRE WITHIN.
—WICCAN CHANT

You won't always be motivated, but you can always have discipline.

A BEAUTIFUL THING
IS *never perfect.*

—EGYPTIAN PROVERB

The best way to forecast the FUTURE is to CREATE IT.

–Bill Gates

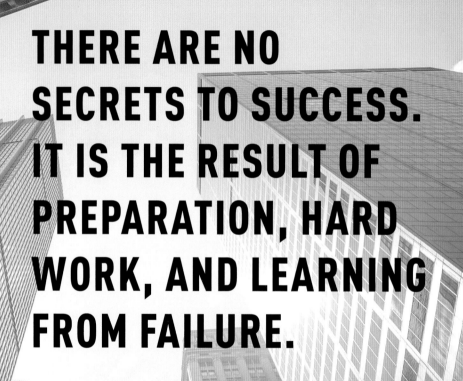

THERE ARE NO SECRETS TO SUCCESS. IT IS THE RESULT OF PREPARATION, HARD WORK, AND LEARNING FROM FAILURE.

—Colin Powell

START EACH DAY WITH A GRATEFUL HEART.

Do more
of what
makes you
happy.

You = Amazing!

Celebrate

EVERY VICTORY,

THE *big* AND

THE *small.*

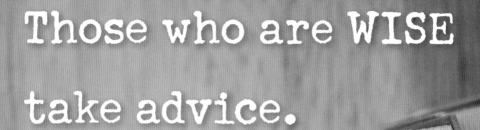

Those who are WISE take advice.

—Irish proverb

Happiness is a warm puppy.

—Charles M. Schulz

BELIEVE THERE IS GOOD IN THE WORLD.

One
happiness
scatters
a thousand
sorrows.

— *Chinese proverb*

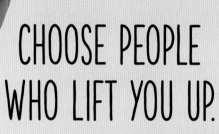

CHOOSE PEOPLE
WHO LIFT YOU UP.

—MICHELLE OBAMA

HARD ROADS OFTEN LEAD TO BEAUTIFUL DESTINATIONS.

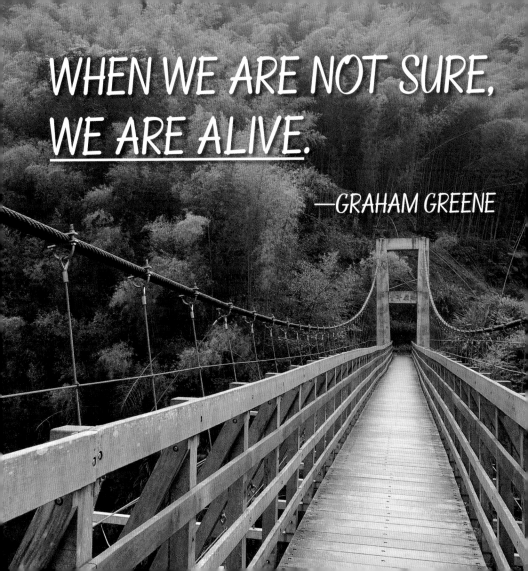

We choose our joys and sorrows long before we experience them.

—Khalil Gibran

FEAR MAKES THE WOLF BIGGER THAN HE IS.

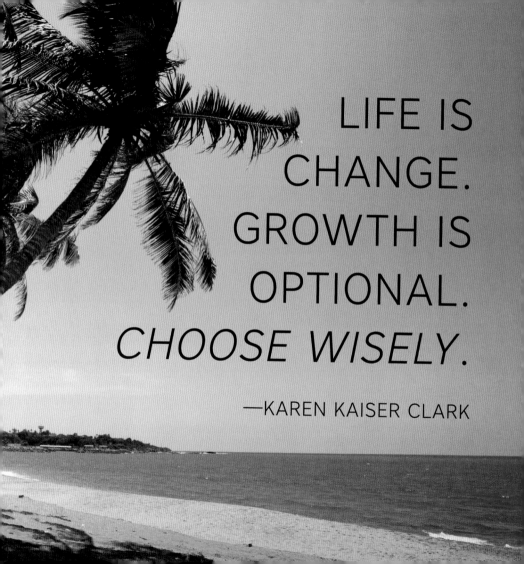

LIFE IS
CHANGE.
GROWTH IS
OPTIONAL.
CHOOSE WISELY.

—KAREN KAISER CLARK

Whatever your hand
finds to do, do it with
all your heart.

—Ecclesiastes 9:10

A SINGLE ARROW IS EASILY BROKEN, BUT NOT TEN IN A BUNDLE.

—JAPANESE PROVERB

A SETBACK IS REALLY JUST A SETUP FOR A COMEBACK.

Turn your
dreams
into plans.

Always believe
that something
wonderful is
about to happen.

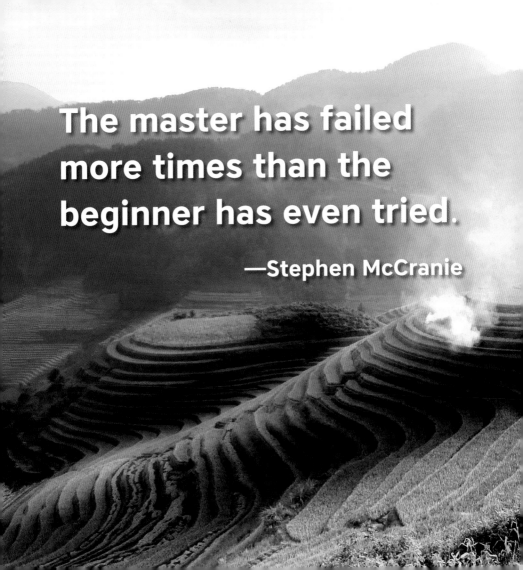

The master has failed more times than the beginner has even tried.

—Stephen McCranie

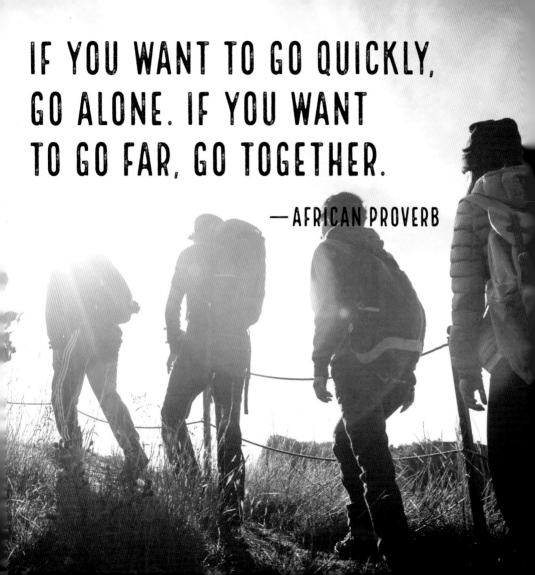

You can't WAKE someone who is PRETENDING to be asleep.

If there
is no wind,
ROW.

Sunshine all the time makes a desert.

—Arabian proverb

There is no pillow
so soft as
a clear conscience.

—German proverb

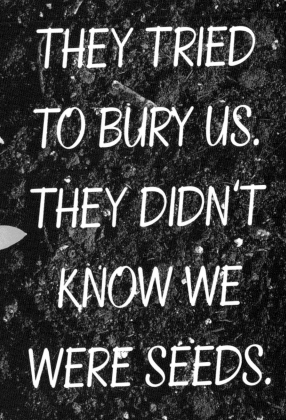

THEY TRIED TO BURY US. THEY DIDN'T KNOW WE WERE SEEDS.

—DINOS CHRISTIANOPOULOS

Happiness never decreases
by being shared.

—Buddha

THE ONLY WAY TO HAVE A FRIEND IS TO BE ONE.

—Ralph Waldo Emerson

Don't carpet the world—
wear slippers.

ASK NOT FOR A LIGHTER BURDEN, BUT FOR STRONGER SHOULDERS.

Buying
what
you don't
need is
stealing from
yourself.

WHEN THE
ROOTS ARE DEEP,
THERE IS NO
REASON TO
FEAR THE WIND.

A smooth sea
never made a
skilled sailor.

—African proverb

Nevertheless,
she persisted.

Image Credits